INVISIBLE REALITIES

Ronald Wright

Revelation Press

© Ronald Wright 2002

ISBN 0 9514038 7 7

All rights reserved
No part of this book may be reproduced
without the written permission of the publisher

Revelation Press
14 Great Innings North
Watton-at Stone
Hertfordshire SG14 3TD

Printed in England by Booksprint

Contents

Introduction	5
What IS 'Spirit'?	7
What IS the 'Spirit World'?	11
The Bible and Christianity	14
The REAL Jesus	19
Origins of the Old Testament	25
The New Testament	30
Hafed spans the centuries	36
The origins of Man	42
Science and Man's future	45

INTRODUCTION

Writing a book about the various aspects of the spirit universe - the realities of the universe, and how it affects the people of this sphere we call Planet Earth is not easy, although the basic facts are quite simple, and there was a time, known as 'The Golden Age' when such facts were common knowledge. The great disruption in the flow between the two universes occurred at that time in human history which the Bible refers to as 'The Fall'. Those affected at that time were not Adam and Eve, but the whole of humanity which they represented.

The link between the two dimensions, despite the disruption, was never completely severed, and those in the finer density sphere we term 'spirit', were able to keep in touch and pass on both messages and wisdom through certain gifted people who we call spirit mediums today.

The purpose of this little book is to explain some of the history of what we now call Spiritualism, and that thing we call 'Truth'. What is Truth? It is the key that opens the door to all the secrets of the earth and cosmos, secrets which our modern scientists misguidedly think only they are capable of discovering,, and although they have made giant steps forward in some fields during the 20th and 21st centuries, they have barely scratched the surface of Truth, for indeed the greatest discoveries that man can make, and must make, cannot be accomplished with the aid of man-made instruments, but only with those gifts and abilities which God has endowed man with, gifts which he seems reluctant to use, largely because of religious ignorance, both past and present, abilities which consequently, sadly, lie dormant and completely untapped in most people, all their earthly lives.

Today when modern society seems to be facing more problems of one kind or another than ever before, and people search for something to give both purpose and meaning to their daily lives, they need to know that they have within themselves all that is required to make the most astonishing discoveries if only they would allow themselves to function as God, the Great Creative Energy Force intended that they should.

You do not have to be an educated person to learn the simple truths, indeed all too often 'clever' people are very materialistic and this can be a hindrance. Jesus pointed this out when he said "Not until you become as little children, can you enter the Kingdom Heaven."

True spiritual knowledgte and awareness points the way for individuals to achieve a fuller development of their nature, mentally, as well as spiritually. It brings an awareness of the purpose that our earthly life has in the universal scheme of things, and thus enables us to fulfill ourselves as the natural law intends that we should do. Our temporary sojourn here on earth should be a preparation for the greater life which is inevitable for us all in the spirit realms.

1
What IS 'Spirit'?

People always fear what they do not understand, which is why present-day churches regard mediums as evil, and scientists regard them as 'nut cases', but the truth is that psychic and spiritual mediums are simply ordinary people whose sight and hearing happens to be more sensitive than most, so much so indeed, that they are able to see and hear beings of a finer density and vibration than the earth's.

Of course mediums vary enormously in quality and ability, and there is a big difference between the psychic who works on the senses, and the spiritual who are sometimes channels for the knowledge and wisdom of teachers who occupy the higher realms of existance.

How many people realise that before being born on earth, they had previously existed in the spirit realms, but that when they were born here, all memory of that past existance was erased from their minds.

The purpose of our coming to the earth is to gain experience such as can only be acquired by living briefly, in the kind of environment that plant earth affords. However, just as someone going into space requires to wear special clothing, or someone wishing to work beneath the sea must have a diving suit, so when we come to earth we need a courser, denser 'shell', in order to adapt to our new surroundings and environment.

Some people may only require to live here briefly, such as when a child dies. The loss of that child, although not understood at the time b y the grieving parents, also affords them certain experiences their spirit has need of, although the law of cause and effect also comes into play of course too. The lessons we have to learn are not always easy, nor are they intended to be.

Compared to our eternal life, our existence on planet earth is extremely brief, even though we may live to a very great age by earth standards, and this is something we need to think about, for we place far too much importance on our brief sojourn here.

As I have already said, our life is eternal, and when we make that transition called 'death', we merely pass from one existance to another. It is like walking through a door from one room to another, shedding or clothing as we do so — the 'clothing' we discard being that material shell of flesh we have 'worn' whilst here.

Here and now, each of us is a triple being — flesh, spirit, and soul. Even children at school these days learn that our earthly bodies consist of billions of molecules, all held in position by electrons — an energy force. What they don't learn however, is that the spirit body is impregnated throughout the material body in that energy force, as in the soul.

Some people may find it difficult at first to believe that a substance which is invisible to most — call it spirit or a ghost, can be a living thing, but what we do actually mean by invisible? We mean something which the eyes cannot see. But bear this in mind, a century or so ago, had I asked someone, even a quite learned person, did a glass of water contain anything other than transparent liquid, they would have replied 'No of course not.' However today we know that if I were to take a single drop of that water, place it on a glass slide and look at it under a microscope, I would see that the tiny drop of 'clear' liquid was in fact teeming with life.

The same can be said for the clear air we breath, and also the clear space that exists between the stars and planets. The truth is there is no such thing as nothing, only varying degrees of density.

Just because the eyesight and hearing of the average person is too poor to register what exists in other dimensions, this is no proof at all that something does not exist.

Likewise it needs to be understood that there is no such thing in this world as a 'solid' object. Stone, steel, wood etc, may appear to be solid, but their structure too is made up of billions of molecules all held in place by an energy force, exactly like our bodies. It is all a question of density and vibrations.

That is the reason a ghost/spirit, call it what you will, is able to pass through what appears to be a solid door or brick wall. Why water will pass through a piece of cloth, even brick given time. You may say well why is it that water will not pass through glass or plastic? It is simply that the molicules that go to make up the glass and plastic, are finer in density than the ones that go to make up the water.

Mentioning spirits who are seen passing through 'solid' objects—shortly after my arrival in the Hertfordshire village where I now live, I was walking along the High Street one morning and suddenly became aware of a man walking towards me. He had the light behind him, and because of this he was just a dark silhouette.

It had been raining earlier, and in order to avoid stepping into a puddle on the pavement, I glanced momentarily at the ground, and when I looked up again, there was no one to be seen.

To my right was a very large, long, 17th century house, and I could only assume he must have entered this while my head had been down. However when I drew level with the front door of the building I could see that the door, and it's handle were covered by a thick layer of undisturbed dust.

My curiosity having got the better of me, I went round to the rear of the building which happened to be a doctor's surgery, and asked the receptionist if the front door was ever used? She replied 'No', it had been locked and bolted for years.

Stranger - to some people perhaps, was a story that came to me in a letter from a friend living in Northwood, Kent. His name is Bramwell Cook, and at the time he was a member of the Salvation Army, and although not believing in Spiritualism himself, he respected my own views and convictions.

The story Bram had to relate was as follows. A friend of his named David who lived in Ramsgate, but who worked daily in Canterbury, was driving home from work one evening in his car along a very quiet stretch of road near Reculver, when suddenly walking along the grass verge ahead of him he saw a young friend named Paul. Since Paul owned a motor bike, David thought it strange that he should be walking along the roadside on foot. Pulling up beside the lad he asked Paul if he wanted a lift? To his surprise the young man replied, "No thank you. I would rather walk."

Reaching home David prepared himself a meal and was just about to eat it when the telephone rang. It was Paul's mother on the line, and between tears the poor woman told him that her son had been killed that afternoon riding his bike along a lonely stretch of road near Reculver! Stunned, David asked what time the accident had occurred. She replied "About 3pm." "But that is impossible" David gasped, "I saw and spoke to Paul on that part of the road around 6pm!"

2
What IS the Spirit World?

Having dealt briefly with the structure of things on planet earth and the universe of the 3rd dimension, let us now consider the universe of spirit, which although invisible to the eyes of most people on planet earth, also consists of matter, but of a very much finer substance than anything we can imagine here on earth. However, to its own inhabitants, the spirit world appears to be every bit as 'solid' as planet earth appears to us.

To illustrate how little the difference between our material bodies and couterpart in the spirit world, it may surprise you to know, that just as we on earth are continually shedding particles of dead skin to be replaced by a new layer, so do we in spirit. So you see even a ghost can have dandruff!

What we call 'death' is in fact only a re-birth, and just as we all have an umbilical cord, that until our birth on earth connects us to our mother, so we also have what is called a silver cord which throughout our life on earth, connects our body of flesh - earthly density, to its spiritual counterpart, and just as the umbilical cord needs to be broken so as to allow us to live in this world, so the silver cord needs to break to allow us entry into the spirit world - so you see how apt is the expression 'reborn'. We don't 'die'. It is quite impossible to die. Life is eternal.

As for the spirit world itself, we are informed that it consists of seven levels or planes - these are the "Many mansions in my Father's house" which Jesus spoke of. Each is of a finer substance and vibration than the preceeding one, and just as we translate from planet earth to the world of spirit at so-called 'death', so in time - many thousands of years, it should be our intention to progress through each and all of these various levels of existence, awareness, and learning.

The average person having led a reasonably good life here on

11

earth, can normally expect to translate to the third level or plane after shedding their earthly shell, and most of the mediums who give you messages from your loved ones in spirit, operate on that level of existence.

One should not make the mistake of thinking however that once you have passed to spirit you have automatically gained entry into what the church like to call 'Heaven'. That level may only be achieved after many hundreds of thousands of years of progression. Indeed the third level of existence, which is normally the 'first stop' for most people, is in many ways not so very different from planet earth.

Plane four is home to many of the wiser spirit guides and teachers who speak to, and instruct us, but the great teachers like Silver Birch, White Eagle, Zodiac, and my own tutor, Prince Hafed, reside on plane five.

The higher we evolve, the less important becomes our individuality, and by the time we reach plane six, we become part of what is called a 'group soul', a 'collective' force, and in our very final stage, we expand still further to become totally absorbed or submerged into that ultimate energy force, that great ocean of bliss which is the Great Cosmic Creator, the Great Universal Intelligence. This is when it can truly be said that we have arrived in 'Heaven', and be at one with that great creative energy force we term 'God.'

At the other end of the scale, those people who through greed or selfishness, have abused and misused their fellow men and women, or led them down paths of corruption in one form or another, translate to the darker regions on plane two.

Murderers and all other truly evil people who have committed crimes against humanity, condemn themselves to plane one, that region which some refer to as Hell or Hades.

It should however be pointed out, that although the behaviour of some may have earned them a place in that darkest region of all, they are not necessarily condemned to remain there for all eternity, contrary to what the Church in its ignorance teaches. For the Great Cosmic Intelligence is an ever-loving force for good, eager for us to repent and progress to a higher level, although it may take many centuries to make such a transition, but there are always those good and noble souls, and Hafed has been one of them, who have volunteered to go down to those darkest of all regions, in a bid to save some discredited soul as a labour of love, for of all things we should demonstrate LOVE is the greatest.

Before ending this chapter dealing with spirit and the spirit world, I would just mention that on one occasion someone once asked me "How big is the spirit world? Considering how many people have passed to it since the beginning of time, it is a wonder there is room for them all!"

The short answer to the question is simply, 'How large is the whole of space?' Hafed once declared that out of curiosity he had attempted to travel to the limits of space, and remarked that although he is capable of travelling through space at the speed of light, he eventually had to abandon the project.

3
The Bible and Christianity

It is claimed that the Bible is still the world's number one bestselling book. This may well be true, for most Christian homes I imagine possess a copy, and a Bible used to be considered a nice 'present' to give someone. But how many people do you know who have actually read even part of it, let alone from cover to cover? The sheer size of it makes this a daunting task, and yet as large as the Bible is, did you know that in its current form it is only a fraction of the original - the UNedited one?

If you do read the Bible, you must accept it for what it is - not the undisputed word of God as certain fanatical religious bodies claim, but a collection of some historical fact, myths, and Hebrew propaganda, the whole being hindered rather than helped by bad translations throughout the centuries, made by men who may well have possessed plenty of religious zeal, but were sadly lacking in true spiritual awareness, and ultimately of course, that should be the purpose of the New Testament at least - to teach spiritual awareness. However in 2,000 years the churches have learned little and forgotten much.

If you are a Christian, have you ever stopped to consider that much of what you follow are not the teachings of Jesus, but the man-made creeds and dogmas drawn up by the Emperor Constantine with the assistance of his aide, Eusebius, some three hundred years after Christ's crucifixion.

At the time of Constantine the Roman Empire extended from the Clyde to the Euphrates and Christians formed a minority of his subjects. They were however a troublesome minority since they were split into three main groups - Orthodoxy which believed that Jesus was devine through and through; Arien who believed that he had a dual nature, both devine and human; and Jesuin which believed that spirit spoke through mediums - spiritually inspired or 'gifted' persons.

Since the bishops of the three factions were constantly bickering over trifles or dogma and constantly ex-communicating each other, they posed a threat to the unity of the Empire as a whole - something which at all costs Constantine was determined to have.

The bishops were asked to submit their views and treaties to him, and when they had all been received, they were promptly burned in an attempt to keep the mass of people ignorant of the varying contentions. Then at the Council of Nicaea in 325 A.D. Constantine made Christianity the state religion, choosing to side with the orthodox bishops and routing members of the other two factions.

Political expediency and nothing else was responsible for Constantine establishing Christianity as the state religion - this was proven by the fact that throughout his life he himself chose to worship the mythical Greek God Apollo. Only as he lay dying did he ask to be baptized a Christian, but as 'founder' he really had no choice.

As a military leader he was greatly admired by his people in the early years, but with the passing of time his extravagant taste for luxury and self-indulgence, and his merciless executions, or murder of those who posed any kind of threat or hindrance to him, can hardly be said to be admirable qualities for the founder of Christianity.

Crispus, Constantine's eldest son by his first wife, was extremely popular with the court, army, and the people, much to the anger and jealousy of Fausta, the Emperor's second wife who wished her own children to have prominence. Ordering the arrest of Crispus, Constantine had his son removed to Pola in Istria, and there a short time later he was put to death.

Grieved by the murder of her grandson, Helena, Constantine's mother, pointed the finger of scorn at Fausta, whose own sons would now succeed to the throne, but far from regretting his actions, Constantine then ordered the murder of Helena, and she was suffocated as she took a steam bath.

Helena had been a devout Christian who in her old age made a pilgrimage to the Holy Land and there, it is believed, found the true cross. Later she was cannonized as a Saint.

Fausta too, in time became a victim of her husband, amongst others. Naturally supporters of the Church will, and do rush forward to defend Constantine - what else would you expect them to do? But the fact remains that he was certainly not a founder to be proud of - more like the skeleton in the cupboard!

The sad fact is, that once Christianity became the official religion of the Roman Empire, real spirituality was pushed to one side, and the 'gifts' of spirit not only ignored but forbidden under pain of death, so that those wielding power in the Church could control the masses, keep them in ignorance, and grow wealthy as a result of their deception.

Throughout history religions have been the cause of so much murder, bloodshed and misery. As is very evident today, religions only divide mankind instead of uniting it. Breed hatred instead of love, intolerance instead of understanding, ignorance instead of enlightenment.

Religious men are rarely spiritual, indeed not only do they often display an ignorance of true spiritual awareness, but a complete inability to comprehend it.

Over the years I have had conversations and correspondence with ministers of various denominations, and always their thinking was bound by the chains of their man-made beliefs. I can recall only one exception, and that was the late Rev. William Butler, a well known Baptist minister who lived at Hornsey, North London.

Bill, as he always insisted I call him, not only 'read palms' for a close circle of friends, but also occasionally accompanied me on visits to the headquarters of the Spiritualist Association of Gt. Britain, in Belgrave Square, for private sittings with various mediums, and it is interesting to note that although he never wore his 'dog-collar' on these occasions, the mediums were always aware that he was a parson.

Once when I asked Bill, "How can you in all conscience continue to serve the Church, when in your heart of hearts you know its teachings are those of men and not God?" Bill with complete honesty replied, "Well I have spent so many years working in the

Church, I am now too old to think about changing my profession. I would not know what else to do. But lets face it, the Church is only a business after all."

Yes, sadly that sums it up - the Church is only a business. The churches do not, and cannot, provide spiritual answers to questions the public might wish to put to them . They don't know the answers, because orthodox Christian religion bans all access to spiritual knowledge.

Why?, because they fear spiritual knowledge. It finds them wanting,and as Rev. Butler was honest enough to admit, it threatens their business and livelihoods. Christianity is materialistic, and the more materialistic we are in this life, the less likely we are to gain even the slightest understanding of Truth.

The search and discovery have to be a purely personal thing. Queen Victoria was one notable person who made the discovery. Her Scots Gillie, the famous John Brown who was always at her side, was a medium, and he it was who kept her in constant touch with her 'dear Albert'. At one time the Queen was keen to publicly declare her belief in Spiritualism, but an angry Arch Bishop of Canterbury quickly pointed out that as 'Defender of the Faith', she would have to give up the Throne if she did.

Another, more recent great believer in spirit was the late Lord Dowding, Air Chief Marshall of the Royal Air Force during World War 11. There is a room dedicated to his memory in the headquarters of the British Spiritualist Association in Belgrave Square, London.

Jesus said himself, and that was 2,000 years ago, "The time is coming when it won't make the slightest difference where God is worshipped. The time is coming, it is here now, when men will worship God in the way He wants - in their hearts and daily lives."

Jesus came to free man from the bondage of orthodox belief, but cleverly while professing to expound the teachings and words of Jesus, still the Church shapes religion to suit its own ends.

Most religious sects, not just Christians, but other world religions also, encourage their followers to believe that unless they

17

follow the doctrines and laws which are laid down, then they are not true believers. This is both nonsense and evil. Men make the pathway to God look so complicated, because they insist in placing obstacles every foot of the way. Learn to recognize the Truth, sweep these obstacles aside, and see the pathway as it really is.

The kingdom of heaven is not a matter of what form your worship takes, nor whether you should or should not eat food on certain days. All such things are superficial. It is your love for each other that is important. Come to know the unity of God, and everthing will be revealed, but if you search only for the fragments (aspects of the one reality) which is what the various religions and churches do, then you will be caught up in those fragments, and where is the unity?

Never compare the differences between the religions for this leads to disharmony. Instead search for the inner stream of Truth that underlies all the religions. God has NO religion, and all the people of the world, indeed the universe, regardless of race, creed, or colour are His family. It is only man who creates the divisions. There is no such thing as a 'Holy War'. Those who seek to create divisions in God's family, or seek to ban links with the Spirit World are the real enemies of God, and the Anti-Christ.

4
The REAL Jesus

A great many books have been written about Jesus over the years. The Bible mentions only his birth and the last four years of his ministry, apart from a brief account of his astounding teachers in the temple at Jerusalem when he was about thirteen and had gone there with his parents to celebrate Passover. His remarkable knowledge and words of wisdom amazed them all. Other than that, the rest of Jesus' life was shrouded in mystery and speculation.

Not so for Spiritualists however, for they are fortunate to have an account of his life given verbally, by no lesser person than the leader of the legendary 'Three Wise Men' who paid homage to the infant Jesus in Bethlehem some two thousand years ago.

The information was given in the presence of eight psychic researchers who were investigating psychic phenomena, between the years of 1869 and 1874. The information, related during one hundred separate 'sittings', was eventually published as a best-selling book in 1875 entitled, HAFED A PRINCE OF PERSIA which received glowing reviews from both Spiritualists and enlightened Christians alike. More than a century later, on the instructions of spirit, I personally revised and republished the book again in 1988.

It is this kind of link, this kind of communication with the spirit world, that is so important to mankind. For the information, guidance, and instruction which such as Prince Hafed are able to impart for our education, is priceless. I do not refer to personal messages from our loved ones in spirit, but information relating to the past, present, and future, of mankind. For they watch over us with great interest, and often alarm.

Prince Hafed himself, was in his later years on earth, Arch Magus of all Persia, and it was in this capacity that he and two chosen companions journeyed to Bethlehem to pay homage to baby Jesus. All three were Zoroastrians, and Hafed himself was a direct descendant of Zoroaster, the great Persian prophet.

The names normally associated with the 'Three Wise Men' - Balthasar, Melchior, and Casper, are mythological since no names were given in the Bible. Their real names however were Hafed, Pacorous, and Cafdraes. All travelled from Persia together.

The Bible tells us that the three Magi were led to Bethlehem by 'a bright star', and there has been much speculation by astrologers as to what star or comet it might have been. However Hafed in his autobiography informs us that the object was neither a star or comet. Here is a description he gives of the event, and the period prior to it —

'Our's was no man-made system. Our wise men, the Magi, received the messages from the altar of the living spirit; they sought to know the will of the most high God, and as they received the response from the altar of the sacred fire they gave it forth to the people, not assembled in a temple built by man, but on the hill-side. There under the blue dome of heaven, we taught of Him who is everwhere - wherever space is, and where is it not? It is far, far beyond the comprehension of man or spirit. There are no limits to the presence of the great king.

'By means of these messages we could also foretell calamities of various kinds that would befall, and gave timely warning to the people so that they might be prepared in some measure to meet them when they did come.

Now, about the time when I came to a thorough knowledge of divine being, so far as it could be attained in the study of the Zoroaster doctrines, I and my true friend, along with another of the brotherhood, received a warning that we had been chosen to receive an important communication in the sacred grove, and that no one else was to be permitted to accompany us. We were also warned that when we entered the grove we were to uncover our heads (not our feet as was the usual custom), to have our sandals on our feet, and, with staff in hand, be ready to execute the mission on which we should then be sent. We could not understand or make out what this warning meant, and we prayed for

God to direct us.

'With bared heads we entered into the dark and sombre grove. On reaching the centre we could not discern a spark of light on the altar - all was dark; the thick foliage of the trees shutting out the still faint light of the morning sun .

'We bent ourselves reverently before the altar, and waited for the coming of the spirit. At length the glowing flame stood over the altar, and grew into the radiant form of the holy spirit which we had so often beheld. Then there fell upon our ears the voice of the heavenly messenger.

'Heaven's faithful servants, I, the angel of the most high, command you to take each one his staff, and at once depart for Judea. There a great and glorious event is about to take place. There the Christ is to be born. He, the long-promised, long-expected one, who is to bless the world with the knowledge of God, and reveal unto men His true character, and ye are chosen to go and bend yourselves in holy reverence before this holy child, the King of Kings, Lord of Lords.'

'This was the message, and when the words were spoken I rose to my feet, and with bended head, thus I spoke. 'My God, as it is Thy will that we go forth to hail the event of him who hath been so long desired, we are ready; and not only to do Thy will in this matter, but to lay down our lives in Thy service. But, where shall we Thy servants find the holy babe? Shall we seek him in the courts and palaces of Jerusalem?

'Nay,' said the glorious one. 'Ye shall find him thus. But I shall be your guiding star by night, and a felt presence by day. There will not be three on the holy mission, but four; for I myself will lead you to the sacred spot. And now, within this holy altar, there are treasures, which you will take with you as gifts to be presented to the new-born king.'

'Treasures,' I cried. 'How came they there?'

'They are the products of earth and air (materialisations). Take them. They are there for you. I know that ye are poor, and unable to provide such costly gems; but doubt not. Take them and carry them to the father and mother of the holy child, for they are poor, and they will yet need such gifts.'

'On coming out of the sacred grove to the light of day, we were greatly astonished to see the assembled brethren fleeing from our presence. We knew not the cause, until we heard the voice of the spirit bidding us veil our faces which had become so dazzlingly bright that our friends imagined we were spirits and not mortals.'

As was quite natural, following their visit to Bethlehem, the Magi kept in constant touch with Jesus throughout his earthly life by letter, and during the 'missing years' in Jesus' life, Hafed informs us that as a boy and youth Jesus twice visited Persia, he also journeyed to India in company with Hafed, and made fleeting visits to both Rome and Athens.

Incidentally, Hafed informs us that Jesus performed his first miracle in Egypt, at the age of six.

All the nations of the Middle East at that time were awaiting the birth of the 'Great Deliverer' who it had been prophesied was to come, but unlike the Jews who expected and hoped for, a military leader who would drive out the hated Romans, the Persians with their more spiritual outlook, knew that Jesus would be a Prince of Peace, who was coming to enlighten and educate mankind, and they were aware that he was, and had to be, no mortal man. Not just another prophet.

So it was, that two thousand years ago the Supreme Cosmic Intelligence despatched to earth that being we call Jesus, in an attempt to re-establish values which had once existed long ago in the 'Golden Age' before mankind 'fell from grace' as the Bible puts it.

Unfortunately however, because of man's rebellious nature and lack of understanding, God's plan was only partly successful, for although during his brief existence here Jesus attempted to restore the broken bridge between the earthly and spiritual worlds, by the beginning of the 4th century, Rome, having adopted Christianity as the state religion, immediately set about replacing all the spiritual aspects of Jesus' teachings, with the more materialistic creeds and dogmas of men, so that in truth, Christianity had become the enemy of the Christlight and not its legacy. So many people, especially religious folk, really have no understanding, even comprehension, of what or who Jesus really is.

To begin with, in appearance he may have looked like other men, but his bodily composition was quite different, for although it was necessary for him to have a 'shell' of flesh in order to survive and function in the harsh environment of plant earth, it was also necessary that he be endowed with those spiritual qualities that demanded that he be born of a virgin, perform miracles, and, when the time was right, dematerialise his earthly shell in a manner that no mortal had ever done, or needed to do, the explosion of the Christ energy creating a lasting impression of himself on his burial cloth - the Turin Shroud as it has come to be called.

Sadly religions not only breed ignorance, but narrow down mankind's vision of Truth, of reality, even in the perception of Jesus. We should realise that he was more than simply the Prince of planet earth - he was, and is, the Supreme Prince of all inhabited planets that exist in space, and there are thousands.

All of these other worlds are superior to planet earth in every way. Religions as such, do not exist, and although Jesus has visited and revealed himself to each and all of them, earth is the only planet that ever attempted to kill him. Proving our absolute inferiority in the universal scheme of things.

Jesus has existed since the beginning of time. Sometimes, even in the Old Testament, he was referred to as 'an angel', at other times as 'a voice'. He it was who in fact gave the Ten Commandments to Moses, although spirit has informed us that those given in the Old Testament are not the original ten.

It was because Jesus had the ability to alter the structure of his form at will, that he was, for instance, able to walk on water as mentioned in the Bible. You will recall that earlier in this book I described how our own bodies consist of billions of molecules all held in place by an energy force, and how spirit is able to pass through apparently 'solid' objects - and to appear quite solid themselves if they so wish.

It was because Jesus was able to assume a body-weight which was lighter than the density of the water, that he was able to walk on its surface. The feeding of the five thousand with a few fishes and a few loaves, is yet another example of Jesus exerting his control of the natural elements, and this is why Jesus said 'greater things than I do, you can do also.' He was telling man that if he was to function fully, with those God-given abilities with which God has endowed him, then truly man could create heaven on earth, which is of course exactly what is asked for in the Lord's Prayer.

Spirit inform us however, that even in the Lord's Prayer itself, mans' lack of spiritual understanding is evident, for when translating the original , one line of the prayer was given the wrong meaning - 'And lead us not into temptation' (as if God would!), should in fact read 'And leave us not when in temptation,' which also makes more obvious sense.

5
Origins of the Old Testament

In preceeding chapters I have attempted to show how from a confusion of thought and deliberate deception, belief in the teachings of Jesus and the Old Testament were manipulated by Constantine and Eusebius who 'selected' what best suited their purposes and burning anything that was in opposition.

Likewise it can be said that the Bible itself is an 'end product' rather than the unique, infallible word of God which it is claimed to be. God is perfection, and since the Bible contains so many contradictions, absurdities, and much that is spiritually ignorant, much of the content is very clearly the thoughts and words of men, not God. We need to sort out the wheat from the chaff. Only then can we gain something approaching the truth.

Please do not think I am trying to destroy your image of what the Bible is or represents - quite the opposite. I merely wish to point out to the reader that some of the deadwood needs to be ignored - clear away the weeds from the garden and you will get a better view of the flowers.

Just where did many of the Old Testament stories originate? Well many people had a hand in writing them as the names of the Biblical books indicate, and some may well have been 'inspired' by the Holy Spirit, it should however be pointed out that in quite a lot of cases the Hebrew accounts of things like the creation and the great flood, bear a striking similarity to myths and stories that abound in other civilisations as geographically distant and diverse as the Mayan and Aztecs of Central and South America, the Buddhist, Hindu, Taoist and Confucian religions, Egyption and Greek mythology, and legends of the Norse and Tahitians.

At first one might be inclined to think that all these other worldwide accounts of the creation, flood etc., add support to the Hebrew version being the original - until you discover that some of their accounts are far older, and this indicates that there was a time way back in the history of the world when there existed an almost universal ancient knowledge - a knowledge which later became fragmented for some reason, yet which still exists in the form of mythology and legends amongst the various peoples of the world.

Unfortunately in the modern world, the word 'myth' has come to mean 'fabrication or fantasy', and the fact that so much ancient mythology predates the written accounts, strengthens the belief of many that this is indeed so.

However, although it would be absurd to accept some of the ancient stories as anything other than a really good yarn to relate round ancient fireplaces in the wintertime, the discovery of Troy in fairly modern times has shown that indeed these stories may well have had more than a thread of truth running through them.

To the group of Christians who refuse to believe that the Bible is anything other than the complete and infallible word of God, I would address this question - Believing what you do, how do you account for the fact that what is called the Bible today, contains only a fraction of the original writings? Who decided which of God's words should be accepted, and which rejected? The answer to that was of course given in an earlier chapter.

The writers of the Bible cannot even agree as to the likeness of God, for in the Old Testament He is depicted as demanding and vengeful, but in the New Testament He is loving and compassionate.

Let us take a look at just a few of the statements in the Old Testament. In Genesis 1/26 God speaks in the plural not singular, saying 'Let us make a man - someone like ourselves'. In Genesis 4/14, Cain, fearing for his safety after killing his brother says - 'Everyone who sees me will want to kill me'. Since the only other people inhabiting the earth were Adam and Eve, why say 'everyone'? The question is also raised how did Cain later 'find' a wife in the land of Nod? Who were her parents?

Perhaps one of the most questionable things in the Old Testament concerns the size of the Ark which Noah built. It was said to contain a pair of every type of animal, reptile and bird on the earth. If this was true, the Ark would have had to be larger than any 21st century oil tanker, and how could Noah have included Bears from the North Pole and Kangeroos from Australia? There would also have been a question of the fish, for salt water fish cannot survive in fresh water, and vice versa.

In Exodus 3/21,22. God tells the Hebrews - 'And I will see to it that the Egyptians load you down with gifts when you leave, so that you will by no means go out empty-handed. Every woman will ask for jewels, silver, gold, and the finest clothes from her Egyptian master's wife and neighbours. You will clothe you sons and daughters with the best of Egypt'.

This was not the voice of God speaking, but the greed of the Hebrews. The same UN-Godly request is repeated in Exodus 11/2. Incidentally since at a later date Jesus would teach against the hoarding of wealth, is it conceivable that God would say the complete opposite?

In Deuteronomy 7/1 and 2, one Hebrew prophet dares to declare - 'When the Lord brings you into the promised land as soon He will, He will destroy the following seven nations, all greater and mightier than you are - the Hittites, the Girgashites, the Amorites, the Canneanites, the Perizziles, the Hivites, and the Jebusites.

'When the Lord your God delivers them to you to be destroyed, do a complete job of it - DON'T MAKE ANY TREATIES OR SHOW THEM MERCY, UTTERLY WIPE THEM OUT',

This was the wish of God who had created all mankind? Never, and history has shown you reap what you sow.

Judges 1/19, gives an amusing and rather ludicrous bit of Hebrew propaganda saying 'The Lord helped the tribe of Judha exterminate the people of the hill country, though they failed in their attempt to conquer the people of the valley who had iron chariots.'

What a pity God was no match for iron chariots!

Perhaps one of the most dreadful acts which God is supposed to have instructed the Israelites to carry out, is given in Samuel 1, 15/1 to 3. This reads as follows - 'One day Samuel said to Saul, "I crowned you king of Israel because God told me to. Now be sure that you obey Him. Here is His command to you.

'I have decided to settle accounts with the nation of the Amalek for refusing to allow my people to cross their territory when Israel came from Egypt. Now go and destroy the entire Amelek nation - men, women, babies, little children, oxen, sheep, camels, and donkeys'.

This sounds more like a command from Adolf Hitler in World War Two, than God. In truth it would seem to be just one more excuse to cover acts of murder and plunder.

In contrast to so many acts of barbarism in the Old Testament, there are, thankfully, a good many accounts of enlightenment trying to penetrate the evil of the time in the form of mediumship.

In Numbers 11/25 for instance there is a description of Moses, who was clearly a medium, having a séance with seventy elders, for we read - 'And the Lord came down in the cloud and talked with Moses, and the Lord took the spirit that was upon Moses and put it upon the seventy elders, and when the spirit rested upon them, they prophesied for some time'.

Numbers 23/5 also speaks about mediumship - 'Then the Lord gave Balaam a message for king Balak', and Numbers 24/2 and 3 also states, 'The spirit of the Lord came upon him (Balaam) and he spoke this prophesy concerning them'.

Perhaps one of the best examples of spirit 'over-shadowing' a medium, appears in Numbers 24/12 and 13, where it states, 'Balaam replied "Didn't I tell your messengers that even if you gave me a palace filled with silver and gold, I couldn't go beyond the words of Jehova, and could not say a word of my own? I said I would say only what Jehova says."

Here is absolute proof that the Lord spoke through mediums - and they are controlled (in some cases) by the Holy Spirit.

In the book of Samuel there are at least two more references of people being used as a link between the worlds of spirit and earth. Samuel 1, 10/6 states "At that time the spirit of the Lord will come nightly upon you and you will prophesy and feel a different person."

'Feel a different person' because a different person had in fact taken over - a spirit from the higher spheres. Yet one more example of a medium in trance.

Then we read in Samuel 1, 10/7 a clear indication that good mediums operate with the blessing of God. - 'From that time on your decisions should be based on whatever seems to be best in the circumstances, for the Lord will guide you.'

I stressed good mediums, because very few top quality mediums are chosen to be messengers for God and those in the higher realms of the spirit world.

As a final example of mediumship being mentioned in the Old Testament, let me quote from Ezekiel 3/27, where God speaking through Ezekiel says - 'Whenever I give you a message, then I will loosen your tongue and let you speak, and you shall say to them; The Lord God says - Let anyone listen who wants to, and let anyone refuse to, but they are rebels.'

Here again is an example of God approving spirit mediumship, and those in the Church who have refused, and do refuse the word from spirit are rebels, make no mistake about it. When they condemn God's messengers, they condemn themselves in the eyes of the God they are supposed to serve.

6
The New Testament

The great mistake that the Jews made two thousand years ago, was in thinking, expecting, that the Messiah when he came would be a great national hero who would deliver them from the hated Romans.

Prince Hafed, Arch Magus of Persia and leader of the legendary 'Three Wise Men' who paid homage to the infant Jesus in Bethlehem, describes the Jewish nation steeped in violence and corruption at that time - 'At its lowest ebb', and adds 'Bloodshed and robbery prevailing throughout the land from the king to the lowest subject'.

It was for this reason, not the occupation of their land by the Romans, that God decided the time had come to send His great representative, Jesus to enlighten them, and it was because they mistook his purpose, that in the main they rejected him.

Later, from the time of Constantine, Christians too would make the mistake of believing that the message of Jesus was solely for them, and not as God intended, for the whole of humanity, and by ignoring the teachings in the purity in which they were given, and substituting them with man-made creeds and dogmas to suit their own purposes, defiled the Truth as it was originally given. This is why a 'Second Coming' is necessary, although this will not occur in the manner which many expect; for Jesus will not return in person a second time to be murdered by the people of earth.

One example of the gulf that exists between the actual teachings of Jesus and what the Church teaches, is given in Matthew 6/5 to 8, where it states 'And now about prayer. When you pray, don't be like the hypocrits who pretend piety by praying publicly on street corners and in the synagogues (churches) where everyone can see them. Truly, that is all the reward they will get. But when you pray, go away by yourself, all alone, and shut the door behind you and pray to your Father secretly, and your Father who knows your secret will reward you'.

'Don't recite the same prayer over and over again as the heathen do, who think that prayers are answered if they are repeated again and again. Remember your Father knows exactly what you need even before you ask him!'

Here is clear condemnation of organised religion, and an attack on so much that the Church holds dear.

In Matthew 23/7 to 9, Jesus says, 'How they enjoy the deference paid to them on the streets, and to be called 'Rabbi' and 'Master' (Bishops and Cardinals). Don't let anyone call you that. For God is your only Rabbi, and all of you are on the same level as brothers. And don't address anyone as Father, (a common practise in the Catholic Church), for only God in Heaven should be addressed like that'.

In Matthew 23/24, Jesus says, 'I will send you prophets, and spirit filled men, and inspired writers, and you will kill some and hound others from city to city'.

Throughout the centuries spiritually gifted and inspired people have been sent to enlighten us, and continually they have been persecuted by priests and clergy fearing the loss of their position and livelihood.

Again in Mark, 12/38, Jesus gives a warning to the Churches - 'Beware of the priests. For they love to wear the robes of the rich and scholarly, and have everyone bow to them - praying long prayers in public. Because of this their punishment will be all the greater'.

In the book of Luke also, Jesus makes very clear the fact that no Church organisation can pass on spiritual truths - only those chosen by him to do so, and in Luke 10/21, 22, he is quoted as saying, 'I praise you, O Father, Lord of heaven and earth, hiding these things from the intellectuals and wordly wise and for revealing them to those who are as trusting as little children. No one really knows the Father except the Son and those whom the Son chooses to reveal him'.

Again in Luke 11/32, Jesus declares, 'Woe to you experts in religion. For you hide the truth from the people. You won't accept it for yourselves, and you prevent others from having the chance to believe it'.

Making very clear what God expects from us - which is not the same thing the Church requires, Jesus says in John 4/21, 'It is not where you worship that matters but how. For God is spirit and we must have his help to worship as we should. The Father wants this kind of worship from us'.

In John 14/6, Jesus declares, 'I am the Way - yes, and the Truth, and the Life. No one gets to the Father except by means of me.'

This did not imply (as the Church suggests), that one cannot enter heaven unless you are a Christian, but that it is important to have spiritual awareness - something Constantine abolished.

However even writers of the Bible such as Matthew, at times showed their lack of spiritual understanding when in Matthew 27/52, 53, he states, '.....and tombs opened and many godly men and women who had died came back to life again. After Jesus' resurrection they left the cemetary and went into Jerusalem, and appeared to many people there'.

The spirit bodies of these people would not have been in their graves, and their physical bodies would have perished long ago.

Paul too, so highly admired by the Church, at times demonstrates an amazing lack of spiritual understanding. For example in Romans 1/17, he says, 'This good news tells us that God makes us ready for heaven - makes us right in God's sight - when we put our faith and trust in Christ to save us.'

Faith and trust in Jesus are not enough to 'save' us. That is something we have to do for ourselves, and Jesus showed us how to - by example.

It is this same blindness of Paul's in Romans 3/25, that results in his declaring, 'For God sent Jesus to take the punishment for our sins and to end God's anger with us.'

It is this same blundering mistake which the Church has nurtured throughout the centuries. If you believe this, then you do not believe what Jesus said himself.

The same ignorance of Paul is repeated in Romans 6/2,3 when he says, 'For sins power over us was broken when we became Christians and were baptized to become part of Jesus Christ;

through his death the power of your sinful nature was shattered.'

What of the non-Christians who have not been baptized? - they are just as much the children of God and part of His creation. Non-Christians who know nothing of Jesus all 'die' just as we do, and all enter the world of spirit just as we do. We get no special privileges for being a Christian. Each finds his/her own way to God no matter which religion they belong to, but it profits Church leaders to try and make people believe otherwise.

In Romans 7/10, Paul states, 'Yet, even though Christ lives within you, your body will die because of sin, but your spirit will live, for Christ has pardoned it.'

Your body will die simply because it is made of perishable material - not because of any 'sin' and if our spirit lives only as a result of Jesus dying on the cross as Paul implies - Who pardoned the prophets and others who had passed in earlier centuries?

Paul again shows his spiritual ignorance when in Romans 8/19 he state, 'For all creation is waiting patiently and hopefully for that future day when God will resurrect His children.' I repeat - who resurrected the prophets of the Old Testament?

Romans 10/3, has Paul declaring, 'For they (the Jews) do not understand that Christ has died to make us 'right with God'.

Christ did not die to make us right with God. He lived to do so.

Romans 13/1,2 has Paul saying, 'Obey the government, for God is the one who put it there. There is no government anywhere that God has not placed in power. So those who refuse to obey the laws of the land are refusing to obey God.

If we are to believe Paul, this means that the Nazi and Communist governments were installed by God!

Corinthians 15/20 has Paul repeating his ignorance when he says, 'But the fact that Christ did rise from the dead, and has become the first of millions who will come back to life,' and in Corinthians 15/21,22, 'Death comes into the world because of what one man (Adam) did. Everyone dies because all of us are related to Adam.'

Galations 3/2, has Paul reprimanding the Galations and saying

33

- 'Let me ask you this one question: Did you receive the Holy Spirit by trying to keep the Jewish laws? Of course not, for the Holy Spirit came upon you only after you heard about Christ and trusted him to save you.'

Men and women have been born with the Holy Spirit since the beginning of time. Jesus' 'death' on the cross merely opened the eyes of people to the Truth. Jesus did not die to take away our 'sin', but to demonstrate the facts.

Jesus did not 'die' to break the power of death - no on can break the power of evil but we ourselves. Earth is a 'classroom' that allows us to encounter evil, and the chief lesson we are here to learn, is how to overcome it for ourselves. If Jesus had 'died' in order that we might avoid the experience, then there would be no point in our being born at all.

Jesus 'died' to free us from the old rules of religion, not to free us from sin. The belief that Jesus did die to lift the burden of sin from us, is one of the most dangerous mistakes which the Church preaches - 'confessions' and 'forgiveness of sins' being in great measure responsible for the sort of thing we are seeing in Northern Ireland today.

Make no mistake about it, anyone, be they Christian, Jew, Muslim, Hindu or any other religion, damn themselves for ever if they think they can murder and do harm to others using religion as an excuse. It can never be justified.

At the moment Jesus died on the cross, the veil in the temple of Jerusalem, which separated the people from the Holy of Holies, was ripped from top to bottom by God, thereby symbolizing that in future there should be NO separation between God and his people. No priests, no religion, only the new set of values which Jesus had taught and demonstrated.

Before closing this review of the New Testament, I would just like to draw attention to a really splendid example of spirit materialisation which is recorded in both Matthew 17/1 to 8, and Luke 9/28 to 35, which is described thus - 'Six days later Jesus took Peter, James, and his brother John to the top of a high and-lonely hill. And as they watched, his appearance changed so that his face shone like the sun and his clothing became dazzling white.

Suddenly Moses and Elijah appeared and were talking with him. Peter blurted out, 'Sir, it's wonderful that we can be here! If you want me to, I'll make three shelters, one for you, one for Moses, and one for Elijah.'

But even as he said it, a bright cloud came over them, and a voice from the cloud said, THIS is my beloved Son, and I am wonderfully pleased with him. Obey him.'

At this the disciples fell face downward to the ground, terribly frightened. Jesus came over and touched them. 'Get up' he said. 'Don't be afraid,' And when they looked up, only Jesus was with them.

The 'brightness of face and clothing' is typical of what happens at such times, and you will recall in chapter 4 how Prince Hafed, when relating how he and two other Magi had been summoned to their sacred grove to receive instructions for the journey they were to undertake, spoke with the Spirit of Light, an angel, and their faces became 'so bright', that as they left the grove other brethren waiting for them outside, fled in terror from them because of their changed appearance. Such is the effect of close contact with those from the higher realms of spirit.

7
Hafed Spans the Centuries.

Both God and Jesus promised that spiritually gifted and inspired people would always be available to channel wisdom, knowledge, and instruction to earth, for the well-being of its inhabitants, and the manner in which time and circumstances are sometimes manipulated by spirit to enable the chosen few to accomplish their tasks, can at times be quite astonishing.

Let me relate a sequence of such events that happened to myself, and began in the late 1960's when on three occasions I narrowly averted death.

In the first instance I had been kicked so violently just above the groin by a drunk, that the muscle wall split and my intestines had begun to seep through forming a visible 'lump'.

My local G.P. and hospital both said that unless I had surgery fairly soon, the tear in the muscles would grow larger, more intestines would spill out, and I would die in terrible agony. However since at the time I was a professional life model, I knew that scars would end my career. When I mentioned this to my doctor he replied 'Which is more important, your life or your career?'

A friend suggested I go to a spiritual healer, and I went to see a lady in Hove. She proved to be a charlatan, but undaunted I went to a second healer living in Aylesbury, who to my great delight was a true channel for healing and was able to repair my damaged body in minutes, and although at no time did his hands make contact with my body - they hovered some four inches above, I DID actually feel my intestines being moved about by unseen hands. It was an eerie experience.

So grateful was I for having my body perfectly restored, I made a pledge to God that should I ever be given the gift of healing myself, then I would do for others what had been done for me.

Not long afterwards I found I DID have the gift, and in the years that followed was able to heal not only humans but many dear animals also.

Then in 1971 whilst on holiday in Corsica and motoring down a very rough mountain road with a companion, both the steering and brakes of the car failed, and we found ourselves racing downhill towards a sharp bend we had no means of negotiating. In seconds we had reached the bend with no protecting wall to stop us plunging thousands of feet into the gorge below.

My companion flung open his door shouting 'Jump' as the front two wheels and bonnet were already going over the edge. I was too frozen with fear to move, but at that very moment the floor of the car was pierced by a sharp piece of rock which held the car firm so that I was able to scramble over the back of my seat and get safely out of one of the back doors.

Just three days later whilst walking along a lonely sandy stretch of beach up to my neck in the sea, the ground suddenly gave way beneath my feet and a strong current quickly carried me out to sea. Not being able to swim, I had been foolish to venture out so far.

Vainly shouting for help, I fought frantically to keep my head above the waves, and swallowing a lot of water I felt I must surely drown, but suddenly when I was about half-a-mile from the shore I felt an arm about me, and heard a voice telling me to relax.

Some time later I was pulled ashore by my unknown rescuer, who after making sure I was all right, walked away before I could even thank him. As I lay on the beach recovering, I wondered WHY in such a short space of time my life had been spared on three occasions. Did spirit have some special mission for me to fulfil?

It seemed they had, for towards the end of the following year, 1972, I had a private sitting with a well known North country medium, the late Minnie Bridges, and having gone into trance, Mrs Bridges began to speak but seemed to have difficulty in finding the right words to say what she wanted to. Then she went into an even deeper state of trance and was taken over by a male entity who explained that since Mrs Bridges seemed unable to pass on the message that was intended for me, he had taken it upon himself to speak to me 'direct'.

I was told that my communicator was 'The Spirit of Light' and that I had been chosen to 'help' in the writing of a 'most important book'. I had never written anything in my life, and so was puzzled by the expression 'help'.

The spirit also declared that I was not only to heal and write, but to teach, saying, 'You are a messenger. You have got to prepare the way for others to follow, and you will be guided, guarded, and instructed step by step'.

I was also told that when the time was right, I would meet 'Three men dressed in black whose names will be Frank, George, and Arthur, one of whom will direct you on the pathway you are to tread'. The spirit also said that although not Jewish, my symbol must always be a 'Star of David surrounded by a ring of bright light'.

A few months later, through automatic writing - my hand writing of itself independent of my mind, I suddenly produced a page of condensed wisdom.

Seeking the advice of my Baptist minister friend, Rev. Butler (who I mentioned in chapter 3), I was told to use my own spiritual awareness to dilute and expand this wisdom so that it could be made available to the public.

Having done this, I produced a little 32-page booklet which I financed out of my own pocket, and which I gave away free of charge to members of the public. Wrongly I was to assume that this automatic writing had fulfilled the prophecy that I would 'help' in the writing of a book.

It was also around this time that Rev. Butler was to mention one day that every time I had called to see him recently, he had observed a bright 'Star of David' shining over, or even resting on top of my head, and said this was a clear indication that I must have some special mission.

It was also while the little booklet was in the process of being printed that I was to actually encounter the three predicted 'Men in Black', which took place in the church of St. Bartholomew the Great, at Smithfield, in London, where I went each weekday to pray for patients on my growing healing list.

To my astonishment their names were Frank, George, and Arthur, and one of them mentioned a book I should try to obtain and read entitled 'Hafed, a Prince of Persia,' although my informant added that because the book was now old and rare - it had been published in 1875, it might take me months, even years before I could locate a copy.

Less than one hour later, seated in my London office, I received a telephone call from an old friend from the North I had not seen for years. He rang to say he was in London for the weekend, and could I meet him next day, Saturday, for a meal and a chat?

The following day, with no intention of looking for the book, we met as planned outside of the Tottenham Court Road underground station, but instead of going to Notting Hill Gate as we had intended, we found ourselves walking down Charing Cross Road, a street famous for its bookshops.

As a result of this, I did make enquiries at every single bookshop in the road, some seventeen in number in those days. However, because by now I had forgotten the title of the book, and did not know its author or publisher, none of the shopkeepers were able to help me. The only thing I could recall, was that the book was about a Persian Prince, which was of no help at all.

I was just about to give up the search for that day, when suddenly we turned the corner into Cecil Court, and seeing yet one more bookshop I went into it. Again the shopkeeper had no idea what I might be searching for, until suddenly I found myself declaring "It is about the missing years in the life of Jesus."

Not knowing what the contents of the book might be, I was astonished that I should utter these words, but hearing them, the shopkeeper responded, 'Ah, then I think I may have just what you are looking for,' and disappeared down into the basement.

Returning a few moments later, the man said, 'It's a very odd thing. I have worked with books for over forty years and had

39

never heard of this one, 'Hafed, a Prince of Persia,' but just a few minutes ago a man walked into the shop with it and said 'You must buy this book from me: it's about the missing years in the life of Jesus' - the same words you just uttered.'

Indeed, so recently had the book been brought into the shop that the man who had sold it, was still there, and the shopkeeper pointed him out. Later I wished I had spoken to the man and asked what had prompted him to sell the book at that precise time.

Clearly spirit was determined that I should have the book ....and their timing for its delivery had been perfect.

Once I had found time to read the book, I knew that this was the one that spirit wanted me to deal with. The language of this Victorian book was out-dated. I must edit it and abridge it for modern readers, and yet preserve the beauty of its narrative. Eventually my version went on sale in 1988, and has been selling ever since.

That however, was not the end of the story, for while Hafed's autobiography was actually in the process of being printed back in 1988, Hafed was to superimpose himself over my body while I was taking a Sunday service at my local Spiritualist church in Hertford.

At first I was not aware of what was happening to me, I only knew that something prompted me to put to one side the sermon I had intended to give, and had spent all the previous day preparing, and whilst my mind was questioning this action and wondering what on earth I was going to talk to the congregation about now, suddenly my tongue started to give the most eloquent sermon of its own, as I stood dumb-founded listening to it.

When my tongue had finished its sermon, I sat down, and as I did so, our guest medium for that day, who had been sitting beside me, turned and asked, 'Do you have a Persian guide? - Only just now as you were talking, a beautiful blue turban appeared on your head, your beard appeared to grow longer and turn white, and you became clothed in a dazzling white robe.'

Open-mouthed I recalled that in Hafed's dictated autobiography which I had been working on, there was a passage in which he had declared that, 'As I grew older and my beard turned white, my favourite attire was always a blue turban and a white robe.'

A wave of emotion passed over me as I became aware that it had been Hafed who had given the sermon that day! Indeed it was to be the first of many that he would give through me after that, proving how fortunate some spritualists are to receive guidance from such exalted beings, whilst those in the orthodox churches are banned from listening to such as this.

Hafed was also to dictate another book - of his Teachings, during the early 1990's, with which he wanted my co-operation , and this was published in 1998 under the title of *A NEW SET OF VALUES*.

8
The Origins of Man

Although the Bible would have us believe that we all descended from Adam and Eve just a few thousand years ago, modern archaeologists are forever making discoveries which raise increasing doubts and speculation as to the facts of our real origins.

Since archaeologists study only the physical side of our evolution, as do scientists probing space with their man-made instruments, even with their most up-to-date technology they have barely scraped the surface of the mystery.

Even the great sages in the spirit world with ancient records at their finger-tips, are not in full possession of all the facts, or if they are, they are not prepared to disclose them.

Prince Hafed however, has informed us that like many of the people who inhabit planets throughout space, our ancestors did not have the same coarse-density bodies which we 'wear' today.

There was a time when the density of our bodies was of the same quality that we only achieve now by 'dying' and casting of this coarse shell.

This shell which we wear today was the result of man 'falling from grace' as it is called in the Bible, symbolised by Adam and Eve in the Garden of Eden. - that paradise-like world that humanity had previously occupied.

As I mentioned at the beginning of the book - out there in space lie worlds and universes such as man cannot imagine. All of a finer density and vibration to this universe which is visible to our weak eyesight, and there was a time in man's distant past when we too inhabited that superior existence.

So superior are the beings that inhabit that level of life, that when they wish to progress to an even higher level still, unlike us on earth, they do not have to 'die' in order to free their bodies from the confines of a denser shell. They simply decide when they are ready to make the move, informing their loved ones of their plan, and then depart just as we would if we were going to emigrate to another country.

Another advantage they have over us, is the fact that whereas when our relations wish to return to visit us from the spirit world we are rarely aware of their prescence, on those higher levels of existence they are able to return in the same density of body, which means they are able to see and to speak to their relatives just as they were able to before 'moving on'.

There are those on earth who believe in reincarnation, but if we are to be logical, we need to ask why, when one has the opportunity to progress to higher and higher levels of finer density, a person would want to keep returning to such an inferior existence on earth?

As with any kind of education, we can only improve ourselves by going forward, not backward, and when the question was put to Prince Hafed, 'have you, in your long experience of life in the spirit, ever met with an individual who had rememberance of passing through more than one existence on earth?' He replied, 'No. If such were the case, I could not say I was myself. I believe I never was on the earth till I was sent direct from the great and mighty source of all spirit. Some men in the spirit world go back to earth, in spirit, and teach those old doctrines they held in mortal life, and which they tenaciously hold on to, but let such men come and stand on the same platform that I and others occupy, and they will soon learn to think otherwise. Many of us do indeed return to earth on errands of love and truth, but not in the body.'

The cosmic intelligences tell us that in the very first instance, before our 'fall' (rebellion against the great Cosmic Intelligence) we too, lived not just in a different density, but on a different planet - it was our changed nature and composition that required we be 'shipped' to the coarser density of planet earth, which we began to colonise some 300,000 years ago.

Gradually these earliest earthly ancestors developed great cultural and scientific cultures which surpass anything which exists on earth today. This was the time known to man as 'The Golden Age' when Atlantis and Lumeria existed.

However, 50,000 years ago these people grew too clever for their own good. Much like the people of the earth today, they grew arrogant, greedy, selfish, and complacent, caring little about each other, the animal kingdom that had been entrusted to them, or of Mother Nature herself.

Not content with this, their leaders genetically interfered with the DNA systems of the populace, reducing the strains in order to make the people less conscious, and more subservient to their new masters. Soon they even began to challenge and doubt the existence of the great Cosmic Intelligence which had created them, so that eventually they destroyed themselves.

Many civilisations have come and gone since that time, and evidence of the oldest of these has yet to be discovered by archeologists. Man is still so ignorant about his past. The garden of Eden as described in the Bible being a myth, a way of communicating facts to simple minds, and Adam and Eve symbolised the human race, their Fall illustrating the destruction of humankind which occurred at that time.

In the ancient world, as in the Middle and Far East even today, stories are a favourite way of teaching people. However, as low as humans were to sink at one part of their history, there was never a time when men and women were on earth in the form of Apes as Darwin supposed.

Eventually, 2,000 years ago, the Supreme Cosmic Intelligence despatched to earth that being we call Jesus, the Christ, the Light Bearer, but men in their ignorance tried to kill him, and God's plans were only partially successful, for although during his brief existence here, Jesus attempted to repair the broken bridge between the spiritual and earthly worlds, we have seen that by the beginning of the 4th century, Rome, by adopting Christianity as the State religion, immediately set about replacing all the spiritual aspects of Jesus' teachings, with the more materialistic creeds and dogmas of men.

9
Science And Man's Future

Some people may feel that in the 21st century, science has replaced the need for God, but I have yet to see the scientist who can create THE life force, or even explain what it is, although of course science is quite capable of exterminating us in our millions, as it is in the process of doing in one way or another at the moment. The warning signs are clearly all around us, and have been for the past thirty odd years, but short-sightedly humanity because of greed, selfishness, and compacency, chooses to ignore them.

We live in an age of silicon chips and computers, where people are fast being replaced by machines and robots. Where animals and poultry are referred to as 'products', and where nothing is natural anymore. Science must try to 'improve' everthing. But slowly mankind is coming to the realisation that hand in hand with so many so-called 'improvements', come a whole range of nightmare side-effects.

We poison the crops, water supplies, and ourselves. We pollute the land, sea, and air, so that every hour three species of wildlife, bird, or insect, are wiped from the face of the planet for ever.

We destroy the rain forests causing landslides and floods, create a hole in the ozone layer that grows ever larger and threatens crops and plant-life as well as increasing cases of skin cancer, and also results in global warming so that the melting ice caps cause sea levels to rise and will in time flood cities like Venice, Amsterdam, and even London. The Thames Barrier will not save London.

For the first time in 150,000 years the icy wastes of Alaska are thawing so fast, that we can expect disasters like Honduras,

Venezuela, Bangladesh, Sudan, and Malaysia etc., to become regular occurrences.

One has only to look back over the past twelve months to see the great changes taking place in temperatures, earthquakes, floods and ferocious storms, even across Europe.

Some of the things mentioned are the result of man's irresponsible behaviour, but there is the additional factor that the planet's land masses and climate do undergo global changes every 26,000 years, and the higher realms of spirit inform us that at this very moment in time, we are in fact coming to the end of the current cycle, which is due to climax around the year 2012.

Politicians, industrialists, and economists talk glibly about changes to our lives in the next 100 years, little realising that in little more than one decade the planet as we know it today, will no longer exist.

At the international environmental conference held in Kyoto last year, to discuss the consequences of global warming - only one of the urgent problems facing humanity, the richest nation on earth, the U.S.A., out of national self-interest, adopted the attitude of 'Blow you Jack I'm O.K.' and made only token concessions, despite the fact that with only 4% of the world's population, they are causing 25% of the pollution.

Normally the U.S.A. is anxious to take top position when it comes to world leadership, but NOT apparently when it affects their own very comfortable lifestyle. When however terrorists caused havoc in New York by destroying the twin towers of the World Trade Centre, the Americans were very quick to demand that the rest of the world stand 'shoulder to shoulder' with them in the fight against terrorism. A clear case of double standards. Truly do people, and nations, reap what they sow.

The Americans, more than anyone, should be setting an example for others to follow. If they expect others to stand by them in time of war, then they should be willing to do the same for others in time of peace. Their concessions at Kyoto were too little too late. The greed of the mega-rich industrial companies and big international corporations, as well as the scientists and politicians in their pay, try to lull the general public into a false sense of security and well-being, in order to fill their own pockets with bigger and bigger profits, but the evidence of their folly is clear for all to see, and the dangerous game they play affects the whole of humanity.

It is important that humans come to a knowledge of their true nature, their true composition, so that they can come to terms with both themselves and the wider universe about them. They must understand that HERE AND NOW they are spirit, not merely a mass of third dimensional particles, and begin to live accordingly.

The sooner we start to do this, the sooner will we get our distorted concepts into proper focus. We must learn to live WITH nature, not against it. We must become loving, caring, thinking, and purposeful beings once again, and not the mindless morons that present-day society would have us all turn into.

Today as in the past centuries, humans are dominated by FEAR - fear of losing ones employment, fear of losing ones home, fears of hunger, Bigh Brother, even each other. Our sports display aggression, our movies and TV revel in acts of violence. Sex and bad language are flaunted publicly.

In the Golden Age of ancient times, humanity lived under laws of LOVE, and this is what we must return to - what circumstances will FORCE us to return to, and this is all part of God's plan.

Let me quote you some passages from Prince Hafed's book, *A NEW SET OF VALUES*, which was published in 1998, and which he had dictated some three years earlier -

'It was never God's will that His children should live in misery, poverty and disease. It is always man's will through following the wrong laws, of greed, of jealousy and hatred, that has set these things in motion.

'It is written in the scriptures that the meek will inherit the earth. When you sit and think about it, it looks impossible, for where are the meek now? How long is this going to take - for ever? It is greatly misunderstood, for while the earth is in its present condition, the meek can never inherit it. The earth can never be as God wants it to be.

'But, you know, those words were not said for nothing. For the mystery of them is like the flower and the seed. It is hidden from your eyes, hidden from your mind.

'It is also written, that in the time of Aquarius, the children of light shall be born. If you link the two together, we are speaking about the same thing. We are speaking about the meek who will inherit the earth.

'I have said to you, that the children of light are not babies who are waiting to be born, but those already living. Many have through the wisdom and truth of God captured that meekness, captured that childlike manner once again, as they try to see and understand with their mind's eye, for out of the womb of misery, will be born the children of light, will be born the meek.

'If you have listened intently to some of the talks that I have given you in the past, you will recall I spoke about the change that is to come into the world. I spoke to you first about the great upheaval that must take place, then told you that out of this upheaval would come forth the meek. For those who have seen wars, great terror and fear, afterwards ARE meek.

'I know that a lot of you are too young to have been through the last world war, but I am certain that if you have heard from others who have, that during that time there was a great brotherhood among the nations that were at war with Germany. There was a friendship that grew up between neighbours, and those whom they did not know, that is not abroad today. For they were all willing to help each other. It was because of the calamity and the great fear that was there in those war days with the bombing. Out of that evil they learned to reach into themselves, and found a kind of comfort in that companionship with each other. A kind of meekness.

'That is what creates it, and shows it to man, when he runs amok with his instruments of destruction. Tearing down peoples homes and lives, and bringing them to their knees in fear. When they are able to raise their heads again, it is as one who is humble and thankful to God for bringing them through the night safely.

'I have spoken of a time that is to be. That is greater in fear and destruction than ever before. Those who survive shall be meek.

'It has been said that the Lord Jesus will return again, and so it shall be. And in that time, when that has happened, shall there grow a great bond between all men. There will be a great love enter their hearts, and a great cry to their God for salvation. The time will be as in the very beginning of time, when man lived in a state of being far removed from what you know now. That time when the wise ones called it 'The Golden Age'.

There will be a thousand years of peace so it is written. This is the time I speak of, and this is the time which is to be completely the reverse of the world you know now.

'For in that time, the power that is locked up in a tiny seed of the flower and the trees, shall be let loose, and the earth will be filled with life again. Man will be raised up as friend and neighbour, and will then, in that time, know why they must walk according to the laws of God and not according to their own wants, desires, and greed, which has brought the world to a near catastrophe of total destruction.

'In that time shall they know these things and thank their God that they have been saved from them. For except that it be for God, then no flesh could live on earth.

'There will be a new kingdom that will be raised up. There will be a new order of life, a new law which will stand fast in the hearts of man, and in the mind of man. For the trees shall bear their fruit, and men shall no longer sup at the table with meat, but will eat the fruit of the earth. The birds of the air will truly be free, and fear nothing. For no fear shall be in the hearts of all life in that time.

'This is the time when the lion shall lie down with the lamb, and there shall be no anger between them. Man shall not work for gain, for treasure. Neither shall there be one above the other, telling him what to do and where to go.

'There shall be no government, only the ruler in your heart which will be God. He shall come and dwell with His children, in their midst. That which they work for, shall be each other and not for themselves or anyone else, and the kingdom that they build shall be blessed with peace. There shall be no more of the anguish that exists between man. No more shall there be the rape of children, and the taking of life, for all that will no longer exist.

'Neither shall any man say, 'This house is mine. I own it.' Or, 'I will fence this field and no man shall enter, because it is my land.' All men will know that everything belongs to all. There is no one who owns more than another. But God has given it to all.

'Neither shall man have to strive for food, neither shall he have contaminated land or water, for all will be sweet and life giving.

'It will be a totally different world. A world where neither the heat of the summer will cause your discomfort, nor the harshness of the winter will give you pain. Where disease will be banished, and it shall not be with you again.

'All that is necessary for that better life shall be yours. You will then know what freedom really is. For you will not be tied in one place, and confined in one place, neither shall your mind be inhibited from reaching out and understanding and grasping greater truths than you have ever known before.

'When a man takes a woman to wife, it will truly be for life. Their love will be for always. Their children shall be their blessing, and they shall raise them in the sight of their God according to how God had instructed.

'There shall be no more death as you know it. For when death comes to you now, your body is buried and those who love you are separated from you, because your spirit can no longer be seen. But in that life and time I speak of, because of the spiritual light that will emanate, the physical body as you now know it will take on a different softness, a different texture, and a different density. One that will be more in keeping with the spirit body. One shall not die in the sense that I have explained, but through their progression shall travel on to other parts of God's kingdom. To that higher realm that they have reached and found.

'But they will not leave behind them loved ones who will yearn for them, and have tears for them, and they shall see them no more. For they will be able to be with them at any time, and they will not be separated by the fact that the spirit is unseen, but they will be able to see each other, and caress each other, as always. Therefore death as you now know it, shall no longer exist.

'Man will progress from this earth, and simply go on to a higher realm, returning whenever he wishes to see those he has left, until they, when their turn comes, will also journey on to where he or she is at that moment, in that different sphere of life.

'So my children, I have tried to paint a picture the best I can, of a way of life that is perhaps unbelievable to you, and I cannot in any way say that if you don't believe it I would be troubled in mind, I can only say that some of you here in this room will witness that new world. Others of you will not. So time itself will reveal the truth to you, and realising in yourself that there must be a time to come when all of these things which are promised must come right.'

As Prince Hafed prohesied, a new age is dawning and the old world we knew is already fast disappearing. The next decade will see the most dramatic change in humanity's entire history as we make the changes necessary for man to return to the fifth dimension, and as we have heard from Hafed, this, like a woman giving birth and bringing new life into the world, cannot take place without a great deal of suffering.

This is the time for a great AWAKENING, not through any one spiritual leader who will suddenly appear, but by a spark of awareness, enlightenment, call it what you will, that needs to be triggered-off in each and every one of us individually.

The Christ (light) must return THROUGH us, IN us, and our attempts to establish a new order, a new way of life, a new set of values.

We do not need science and technology in order to make the most astounding discoveries, if we would only function as the Great Creator intended that we should - by using those spiritual gifts and abilities which we all have deep within us, abilities that sadly in the vast majority of people, lie dormant and untapped, all their earthly lives.

The Lord's Prayer asks that - 'They will be done on Earth as it is in Heaven' - that plea, will shortly be granted. Will YOU be ready for the change when it comes?

Other books available from Revelation Press

HAFED — A PRINCE OF PERSIA
Autobiography first printed 1875
Edited and abridged by Ronald Wright 1988 and reprinted 1988, 1989 and 1996

HAFED AND HERMES (the sequel to HAFED)
Life in the Spirit World first printed 1875
Edited and abridged by Ronald Wright 1988 and reprinted 1988, 1989 and 1996.

A NEW SET OF VALUES
The Teachings of Hafed edited and abridged by Ronald Wright 1998.

WHAT DID GOD SAY?   Ronald Wright
First printed 1987 and reprinted 1996.

JESUS—the WHOLE story   Ronald Wright
First printed 1989 and reprinted 1996.

FLESH—the great illusion
Autobiography of Ronald Wright printed in 1990 but now out of print.

HAFED—A PRINCE OF PERSIA

"Dead" for 2 000 years, Hafed relates his own life story.

Every December Christians celebrate the birth of Jesus and remember the "Three Wise Men" who paid homage to the infant and presented him with gifts. The Bible refers to these men as "Kings", but who in fact WERE these men and where did they really come from?

For nearly 2 000 years these questions remained a mystery, but in 1869 a group of researchers investigating psychic phenomena conducted a séance with the Glasgow medium David Duguid, and what resulted was to be one of the most dramatic and important spirit communications since the days of the Old Testament.

An entity claiming to be the leader of the legendary "three" spoke to the group and wished to impart so much information that a total of one hundred "sittings" over the following four years were required. Notes were taken and published as a book in 1875, but all copies of the original having now virtually disappeared, a spirit "voice" instructed Ronald Wright to revive it, and this he did in 1987.

The book gives a fascinating glimpse into the life of ancient times, and reveals aspects of Christ's life not previously known, astonishing knowledge quite beyond the capacity of either David Duguid or anyone present at his séances.

Reviews of the original book of 1875:

'It has an interest for us greater than the contents of any other book outside the Holy Scriptures— all Christian ministers should make themselves acquainted with this book'

(Glasgow Christian News)

'Of the greatest importance`—one of the most extaordinary works that has appeared in connection with Spiritualism'

(The Spiritual Magazine, London)

'Viewed simply as a work of imagination, literature has nothing to equal this marvellous narrative'

(Religio Philosophical Journal, Chicago)

Paperback £5.95
(Add £1 for postage and packing)

HAFED AND HERMES

Autobiographical sequel to *HAFED—A PRINCE OF PERSIA*
In this volume Hafed gives us not only a glimpse into that other world beyond the grave, but answers many questions which have puzzled people of the earth throughout history.

Hermes, a childhood friend and disciple of Jesus, also gives an account of life with the Master, and answers questions.

A book that takes all the fear out of 'death', and gives comfort to those who mourn their loved ones.

Reviews:
'It is a most extraordinary book and deserves a very wide readership indeed—the description Hafed gives of his reception in the Spirit World after his 'death' and his reunion with his loved ones is a very moving commentary on the possibilities that await all of us.'

(Greater World)

'Articulate and thoroughly absorbing.' 'Of particular interest is the question and answer section in the back of the book. Well worth acquiring.'

(Psychic News)

'Containing descriptions of the Spirit World, clarifications of events in Palestine after the Resurrection which make interesting reading.'

(Two Worlds)

'Difficult to do it justice in a review.'

(Unitarian Society for Psychical Studies)

Paperback £5.95
(Add £1 for postage and packing)

A NEW SET OF VALUES
By Prince Hafed — edited and abridged by Ronald Wright

This book was dictated by Hafed, leader of the Three Wise Men who paid homage to the Christ child two thousand years ago.

Hafed declares it was NEVER God's intention that a religion be created in Jesus' name. Religions only DIVIDE mankind."

Hafed foretold the collapse of communism in Russia long before it happened, now he warns that unless we cease to abuse and exploit Mother Nature and change our materialistic, greedy and decadent society, then within the LIFETIME of many people now living, the human race will face almost total extinction. Indeed, the process has ALREADY BEGUN.

With great logic and commonsense Hafed explains the steps humanity should be taking to prepare itself. It is a book EVERYONE should read, for we are LIVING ON A TIMEBOMB.

Reviews:

'I Guarantee that if everyone followed the teachings of this script, this world would be a much better, healthier and safer place to live in. Brilliant philosophy and covering just about every subject you could imagine'

(Psychic World)

'I urge you to read and digest this important and thought provoking book'—'Its message is crucialto each and everyone of us'—'Merits serious study'—'Ronald Wright's commentary is eloquent, perceptive and prophetic'—'It desrves the closest scrutiny'

(Two Worlds)

'Sublime wisdom and unmatched enlightenment'—'Humanity cries out for such VALUES'

—'Essential reading for everyone, and I do mean EVERYONE'

(New Horizons, USA)

Paperback £7.95
(Add £1 for postage and packing)

What DID God Say?
Ronald Wright

Not a book for the bigoted or narrow-minded— but those who seek true enlightenment.

Is the Bible really the infallible 'voice' of God? Are the creeds and dogmas of the Christian Church in direct conflict with the teachings of Jesus? What does the Bible really say about mediums and spiritualism? Is Jesus really God? Can priests forgive sins? Did Jesus really 'die' for our sins? Is man made in God's image? Are churches or priests really necessary?

The answers to all these questions are in the Bible, but they are NOT the ones given to the people by 'The Church'.

It is claimed that the Bible is still the world's number one 'best-selling' book and this may be so but it is also the least understood book ever published.

In this small volume the author not only deals with the above questions but also comments on many of the contradictions and absurdities contained in the Bible.

The author also gives helpful enlightenment on questions relating to some of the 'mysteries'— mysteries which can only be explained by someone possessing true spiritual awareness. A well-known Baptist minister, the late Rev. William R. Butler of Highbury, London, once said of the author, "He has been given spiritual insight not given to all".

Review:

'A drastic break with tradition'...'Sounding like an exasperated cross between Alf Garnett and A..L.Rowse, Mr. Wright disparages the Bible's original scribes'...'this fascinating volume'
(London Evening Standard)

Paperback £3.50
(Add 50p for postage and packing)

JESUS the WHOLE story
Ronald Wright

There have been countless books about the life of Christ, but this one is different in that it accounts for those tantalising 'unknown' years BEFORE his ministry began, which, blended with a single narrative of the four Gospels, gives a more complete picture of Christ's life than has ever been attempted previously.

Reviews:
'If someone who was not a Christian wanted to know about the life of Jesus, here is a very readable book which tells the story in an understandable way — ideal for a Muslim, Buddhist or Hindu who wanted some idea of what the Christian story is. This little book is not likely to be found on the book-shelves of a theologian — a good reason for reading it'.
(Churches Fellowship for Psychical Studies, Scotland)

'This fascinating book is well worth reading'...'The timeless appeal of the publication perfectly captures the atmosphere of the time in a way lacking in many other publications on the subject'.
(Psychic News)

'It deserves a place on any serious readers bookshelf'
(Greater World)

'Gives a more complete picture of Christ's life than has ever been attempted previously'
(Spiritual Gazette)

Paperback £5.95
(Add £1 for postage and packing)